Fairchild's book
of window display

Fairchild's book of window display

by SHIRLEY JOEL

Fairchild Publications, Inc., New York

contents

foreword

Ideas for window display come from everywhere. Including books on window display. Thus this visual report on recent trends in retail store window display from all over the world.

As a comprehensive view of current approaches to window display, with particular emphasis on fashion, furnishings, and seasonal presentations, its objective is to inspire, stimulate and inform all those display people now, or soon to be, behind the scenes of window display.

While neither a how-to-book on the techniques of window display (although some "tricks of the trade" are explained in a later section), nor a round-up of the "best," "most unusual," "most anything", every display shown does meet professional standards of competence, artistry and imagination, offering a high quotient of inspiration and ideas. And few, whatever their achievements in merchandising or window design, can ever have enough of those.

introduction

THE POWER AND THE PERSONALITY

The buyer fights for them. Manufacturers knock themselves out for them. Even customers have been known to go out of their way for a rewarding glimpse of them. Such is the power of store window displays.

Not only is the store window and the presentation of the merchandise in it one of the single most powerful selling tools today, but it is also a strong reflection of the store within; the tipoff to current and potential customers of a store's personality and philosophy . . . something this is frequently overlooked by both store management and display designer.

It's not the merchandise alone nor the price that fixes the store's image in a customer's mind. The way that merchandise is arranged, presented, displayed—call it what you will—sometimes reveals more about a store than a day-long shopping excursion within its walls. Is the store original? Interesting? Witty? Does it show a taste for good art? A flair for the unusual? Is it friendly or formal? Casual or conservative? The window display can frequently tell all. By the adroit use of a prop. Or a malaprop. Even though the merchandise plopped in the window is new, and knockout. Whatever philosophy or personality a store would like to project, it can and should project through its windows. Just as window display people take great pains to integrate the physical aspects of the window with the store facade, so must they integrate the psychological overtones of the window arrangement with the total personality of the store.

It is important to understand the store, its goals, and the kind of customer it hopes to attract. Get too "uptown" with a promotional window and you may lose the customer you'd like to lure. Pull in the same old tacky Louis XIV chair as background for a couture ballgown, and you turn off a different customer.

The whole idea is that each article of merchandise needs a setting appropriate to its appeal and the store that sells it. Small store owners (who frequently do their own window displays) may shrug and say that it's all well and good when there's a big budget to play with. Then one can afford to have things made-to-order, do research, buy fancy props. But it's a funny thing. Frequently, it's the big store with the big budget that fails to come across to the public with a clear and appealing personality. Perhaps its very bigness muddies the image. Maybe too many messages are being sent at once. Here, the small store has a decided advantage. It's forced to be spare and inventive—that is, if it wants to put an attractive window forward. And in so being, it creates an attitude that is often off-beat, consistent, and highly individual.

WHICH COMES FIRST—THE MERCHANDISE OR THE IDEA?

The merchandise is pivotal. That's where it all starts. Frequently, the buyer of a store department, or the store owner will work directly with the window display people in planning windows. Or the merchandising group may select what they want to show

and then the display designer edits the collection and takes it from there. But one thing is sure. Merchandise that goes into a window, whatever its category, should be new and newsworthy.

Every so often there is an occasional misguided merchant who thinks he can push the "dog" of the season—the stuff he can't give away—by putting it in the window. Which is too bad. A gross waste of valuable window space. When customers know the merchandise and have already rejected it, why show it?

Just as newspapers put their newsiest items on the front page or give them bold display type, so should a store reserve its front and key displays for "hot off the press" items. That's what keeps a store in the news. Moreover, there should be sufficient stock behind a window display for those who come in to try and buy. ("Sorry, the only size 10 is in the window" is not exactly conducive to good customer relations.)

Sometimes the merchandise and the idea for its presentation seem to be born simultaneously. Alert window designers who keep current with what's happening in clothes, furnishings, food, literature, lifestyle, are almost always visualizing different articles with a variety of new props and settings. Because they are tuned into trends in all areas and often cover the resources where the merchandise is produced, they spot potential good window material early, and may make suggestions to the buyers, even before the merchandise is ordered. Already in the designer's head is the idea for dramatizing nostalgic fashion by using an amusing "thrift" shop motif. Or the display person may have spotted some bright new avant-garde art that would be perfect for incoming chrome and glass furnishings. Certainly, the merchandise comes first. But close behind it is the idea that's going to set it off or frame it.

WHERE DO WINDOW IDEAS COME FROM?

Well, once again let's start with the merchandise. What's it made of? Animal, vegetable, mineral? Look to the material of the merchandise and consider it as background, individual prop, or in its raw state. Copper, brass, silver; plaid, burlap, canvas, cotton. Any possibilities there? And consider the color. Not only of the articles shown, but also their complimentary, contrasting, and clashing colors. Clashing can be smashing, if used with care. Price can inspire an idea. (See the Delman Shoe Final Clearance in the accessories section). Even signs can platform an idea. Again, note in the windows shown how different stores show price and window copy with interesting little hands, signs, posters. Style and use may pre-determine many a window direction, but they do not necessarily limit their inspiration. High fashion often is the most exciting in incongruous settings. So is fine jewelry. In fact, the more costly and the more incongruous, the more exciting. How is the thing made? Is it worth taking apart and dramatizing an "exploded" view? That goes for clothes, too. Maybe some fresh new seaming, sleeving, shaping, calls for some interesting analysis that not only helps educate the customer, but also merchandises the news of the construction.

The whole idea is one idea at a time. Keep it simple. That doesn't necessarily mean eliminate merchandise; just a multiplicity of conflicting ideas. Less is more, according to Le Corbusier. And never more so than when you seek to project a feeling of elegance, class, sophistication. On the other hand, nothing can be more dazzling than a window spilling over all kinds of goodies so that every corner holds still another delight. The Christmas fantasy gift window is a prime example. Which is the source of another idea. The season. Tie in with it. Or tie in with the town. What's happening in your little village, city, country? Social, cultural, ecological, sociological, illogical? The trappings of wealth, health, and happiness change as fast as the fashion does. Merchandise doesn't exist in a vacuum. Neither should the store window. Neither should the window display designer.

1. accessories & cosmetics

1. accessories & cosmetics

Too often, accessories and cosmetics are given short shrift by a display department or a store. Usually, these categories are relegated to a small side or vestibule window. Or they are tucked to one side of a major fashion presentation. All of which is okay. Accessories should be tied in with the clothes they're supposed to be worn with. And small windows are a natural for the scale of most accessories. But that doesn't mean they don't deserve a large window with good position some time (and not just at gift times like Christmas). Large windows can be so framed that they pull the passer-by right in. Large open space can often be dramatized to highlight a major motif or provide unusual propping and imaginative background. And of course, lots of air and deliberate open space around a tight grouping of select accessories can speak volumes for the class and quality of the store.

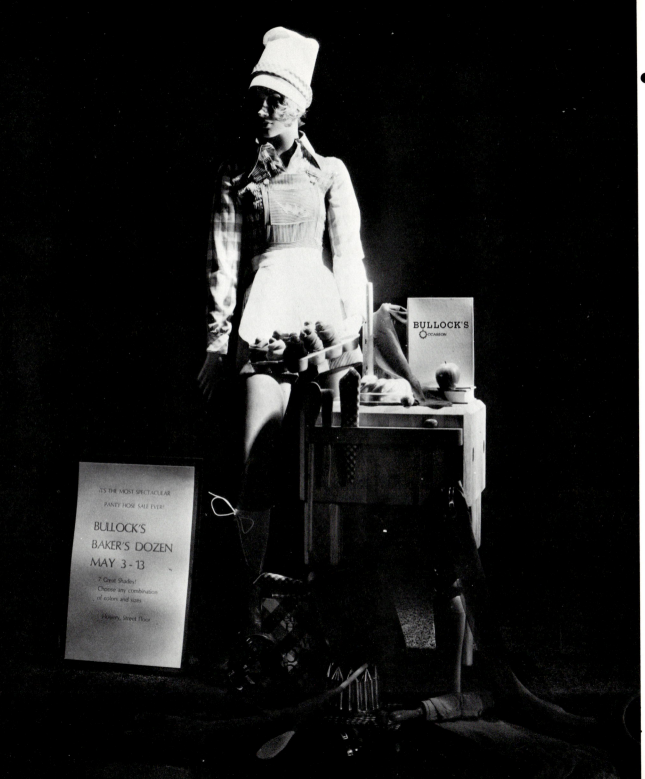

A ● Demonstrating that there is a dramatic way to promote a sale, and a pantyhose sale at that, Bullock's, Los Angeles, capitalizes on the "baker's dozen" idea (13 pair for the price of 12). Thus baking paraphernalia, including freshly-done cupcakes, provide some unexpected props for always-difficult-to-prop pantyhose, as well as an interesting window visually.

B ● Another imaginative way to put across pantyhose—a pantyhose "put-on" by Lipman Wolfe & Co., Portland. A stylized mannequin sprouts some angelic wings—which are actually basic see-through leg forms for stocking display. Clever, no?

C ● If you're going into the reptilian era, it makes sense to hark back to some stark primitive time. Only when Neiman Marcus, Dallas, does it, primitive becomes posh and stark turns out stylish, although the grouping is indeed sparse. It's all a matter of careful composition and one basic prop—the simulated stone.

D ● The delicate shoe obviously needs to be presented with delicacy, without diminishing impact. Bergdorf Goodman, New York, achieves this for its Delman shoe collection by putting the shoes in sand and filling a leg form with water and some unexpected seaweed.

● C

Fantasy tips th

● D

From the
Delman
Collection

E● A compact contemporary grouping of shoes utilizes the line and shapes of modern graphics to focus on the line and shapes of the shoes. The window is open and airy, background is stark black, and the whole thing belongs to John Wanamaker, Philadelphia.

F● Art deco motifs make up a stage-like proscenium with successive "curtains" dropping down to frame a classic grouping of shoes and handbags. I. Miller, New York, is the store.

6

G

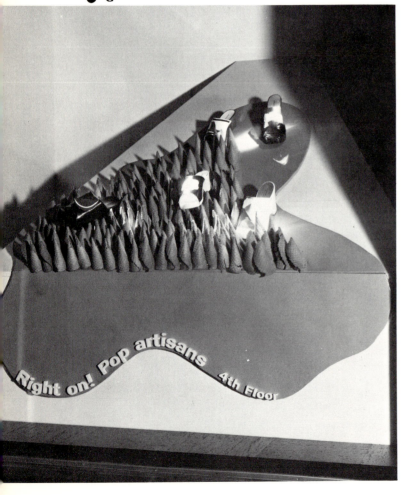

H

...FROSTINGS

● I

G ● There's no end to the way ice cream cones (especially real ones) can flavor a window setting. Bloomingdale's, New York piles them up on mouth-watering pink vinyl and pops some fanciful summer clogs right on top. Background is frosty-white. Nice summer idea—for almost any category of merchandise.

H ● A small window carefully composed to display three handbags, a scarf and belt for Roberta di Camerino, Rome. Note how the scarf is deliberately draped to exhibit the belt motif while providing additional graphic interest for an essentially straightforward display presentation.

I ● A timely and topical way to group accessories for an interior Christmas window, Livingston's, San Francisco. Snowflake designs are screened on plexiglas cubes and window glass, while copy picks up the theme, "Frosting."

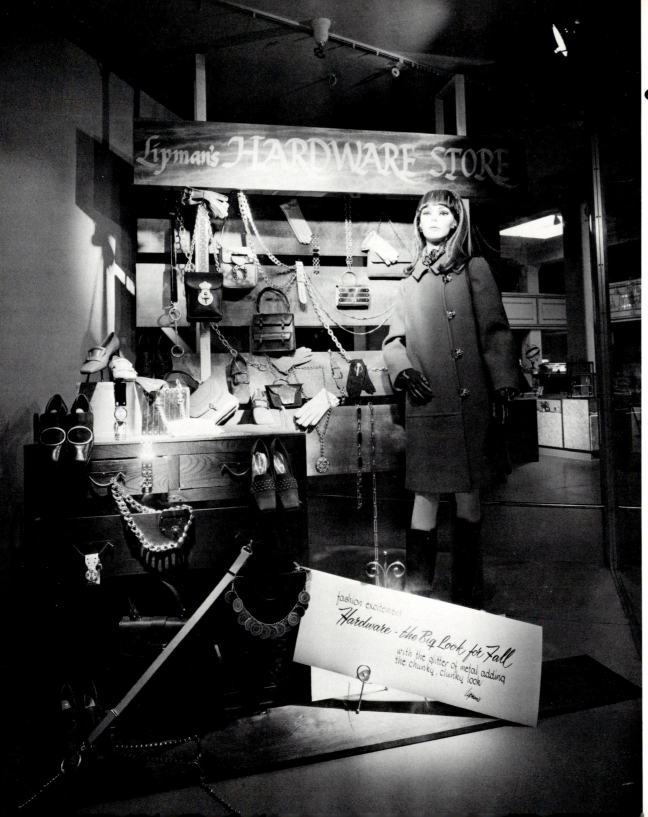

● K

J ● Given a good-size window to work in, Gimbels, Philadelphia, creates a potent accessory vignette filled with gift ideas. The background artwork is done in mauves, pinks and sepia tones against white, to highlight a select group of fashion accessories.

K ● Playing on the "hardware" theme in fashion, Lipman, Wolfe & Co., Portland, frames in a "Hardware Store" with simple wood planks, old-fashioned sign, and a handsome chest. The latter offers interesting display possibilities for almost any kind of accessory that fits the "hardware" category.

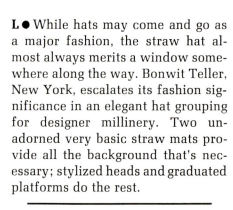

L ● While hats may come and go as a major fashion, the straw hat almost always merits a window somewhere along the way. Bonwit Teller, New York, escalates its fashion significance in an elegant hat grouping for designer millinery. Two unadorned very basic straw mats provide all the background that's necessary; stylized heads and graduated platforms do the rest.

M ● A classic background for exclusive beauty products immediately establishes an atmosphere of quality. The Halle Bros. Co., Cleveland, does it with some simulated antiquity, working in the classic bottle and jar shapes most eloquently.

N ● Cosmetics were an integral part of "The Biba Look from London" (a trendy London boutique collection) that Bergdorf Goodman, New York, launched recently. To establish the thirty-ish mood typical of the collection at the time, art deco shapes and mirrors transform a small window into an intimate boudoir—for a movie star, maybe?

For spring ...what could be more natural than a beautiful straw from Irene of New York! Designer Millinery Salon, Sixth Floor

Macy's
Young Artist
ACCESSORY COLLECTIONS
present

SPECIAL COTY AWARD WINNER
CLIFTON NICHOLSON, WHO
HAS CREATED AN ANIMAL
KINGDOM IN GOLD METAL
AND GOLD METAL WITH
ENAMEL. HIS UNUSUAL DESIGNS
ARE REPRESENTED IN
SEVERAL MUSEUM COLLECTIONS
AND THE MODELS FOR HIS
METAL JEWELRY DESIGNS ARE
DEVELOPED USING THE
INTRICATE LOST-WAX
TECHNIQUE

Accessory Bazaar
STREET FLOOR

O ● Marshall Field, Chicago, introduces a new perfume fragrance by using the brand name, "Infini," as part of the background design so that it becomes a showcase for the perfume and package. Bottles are elevated on shiny silver cubes and the whole effect is modern and elegant.

P ● Belts, part of spring's bounty and opulence, spill out of a charming picnic basket for a fascinating Bonwit Teller, New York, accessory window. Substitute jewelry, shoes, other small accessory items and the window would still work.

Q ● Capitalizing on the increasing appearance of young artistic vendors peddling their wares on the street, Macy's, New York, builds a window around its own artist and his wares. A lifesize photographic blow-up is background to merchandise suspended by wire so that it's hard to tell what's photographed and what's in the "flesh."

● R

Out of the tribal archives

● S

● T

16

 U

R ● The American Indian given the full fashion treatment. Saks Fifth Avenue, New York, does it right with an authentic hanging for background, a chic mannequin got up in harmonizing outfit, and jewelry simply displayed on classic velvet forms set on mirrored pillars.

S ● Mailed fists turn out to be the perfect foil for costly jewelry at Bergdorf Goodman, New York. The window is framed with black, and lighting heightens the drama by focusing in on the jewel itself. Costume jewelry would be equally effective.

T ● Golf tees in a window for very expensive jewels? Cartier, New York, considers them ideal for setting up a jewel of a pin, further illuminated by one dazzling spotlight, so the eye can't miss.

U ● Tiffany, New York, gives viewers the works and winds up with a spectacular watch display. The collage of watch parts is on clear plastic; the technique could easily be utilized to make a statement for the parts adding up to the whole in many other merchandise areas.

2. the boutique approach and small specialty shop

2. the boutique approach & small specialty shop

What has come to be identified as the "boutique" approach in window display is really nothing more than off-beat, non-traditional types of merchandise presentation. Frequently there is an uninhibited mix of merchandise, seemingly unrelated. Mannequins, if used at all, may be of unexpected materials such as straw, chicken wire, abstract shapes of metal piping. Clothes are often draped on floors or walls, suspended from the ceiling, or "fly" through the air with the aid of cleverly manipulated wire.

By breaking with tradition, both in the kind of merchandise carried and its presentation, the boutique and the small specialty shop that is sometimes dubbed "boutique" have developed a highly individualistic look that many large stores now go to great lengths to copy. Thus a look or an approach that once was associated only with a small specialty shop or far-out boutique has been picked up by almost any store that wants to put across a message of adventurousness, unique merchandise, and individuality.

A ● Typical of the adventurous approach the boutique usually takes in its window display, Daniel Hechter of Paris props a motorbike in its window, and proceeds from there, with no attempt to be literal. The mannequin is frankly sexy. Leather pants are flying. Other merchandise is cleverly draped around dis-embodied forms.

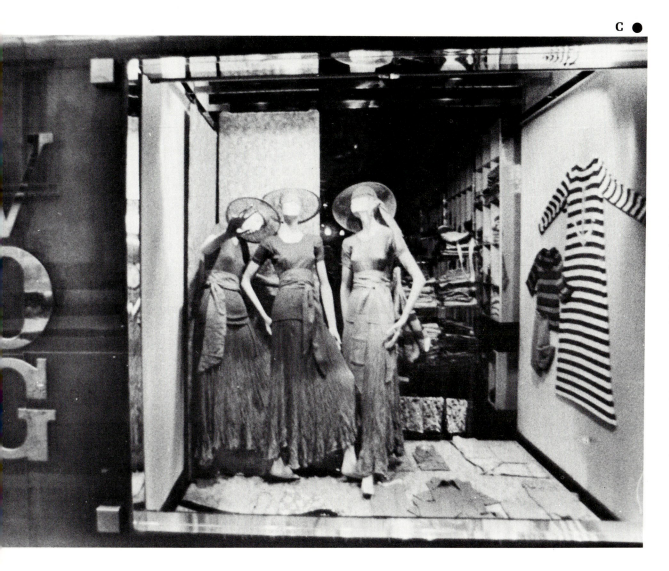

B ● An excellent example of the art of draping that Parisian shops seem particularly adept at; clothes are folded and tacked against the wall of a shallow window for Prisunic, Paris. The cut-out parrot is a bit of whimsy that also reflects the light-hearted spirit of the boutique approach.

C ● Vog, one of the earliest European boutiques, does its Rome window in traditional "non-traditional" boutique style. Mannequins are stark, clearly modern. Walls are used to lay out other merchandise quite flat. More items are spaced about on the floor. In this way, a lot of merchandise is displayed, without benefit of props, in a remarkably small amount of space.

23

D

D ● When a conservative "establishment" store such as Bergdorf Goodman, New York, introduces its own version of a famous London boutique, it may well outdo the original. A bank of six windows, completely black except for the lone color of coordinated clothes and accessories, launched the Biba look for "Bigi at Bergdorf" (aimed at a young juniorish customer). Continuity was provided with a basic clothes-hat rack in each window, and a giant photographic blow-up.

E ● In New York, the Boutique Valentino, taking advantage of a striking multi-storied circular window, uses the floor as platform for a book tie-in. Mannequins are realistic in order to make a strong link with the author, customer and subjects of the book shown. The use of mannequins modelled after real people is probably most effective in a big city where the faces and figures are well-known.

F ● In Rome, the Valentino Boutique expresses both elegance and exclusivity via a paucity of props and clothes draped on the floor and hanger-forms. The lone mannequin wears the most avant hair-do and makeup; is posed in an attitude of haughty nonchalance.

24

Dots
Show All-Time
Dash

TRIBOUTIQUE
ON THREE

G ● There is no rule that says a large store can't adopt the techniques of the small boutique. Stix, Baer & Fuller of St. Louis shows how well they work in a branch store window where clever off-beat design—using newspaper tear sheets and only two mannequins—achieves a feeling of excitement and news.

H ● With wit and great style, John Wanamaker, Philadelphia, projects a feeling of exclusivity for its Tribout Shop, a department within the store that concentrates on top fashion. The stylized mannequin, the choice of dress, the black background relieved only by dimensional cut-outs, are all indicative of the uncluttered look characteristic of the couture specialty shop window.

Ale Schrader chooses the American Way With Wool

I ● B. Altman and Co., New York, captures the mood of a small exclusive specialty shop with a spare window arrangement devoted to a single item. Instead of being shown on a mannequin, the dress is fastened with wire to heavy board and an artist's fashion sketch helps establish a designer theme.

J ● Nothing is static in a carefully composed accessory window for the Rome boutique of Roberta di Camerino. With practically no props save a standing pole, there emerges an animated mix of scarves, handbags, belts and umbrella—against a floor stripped bare and simple walls.

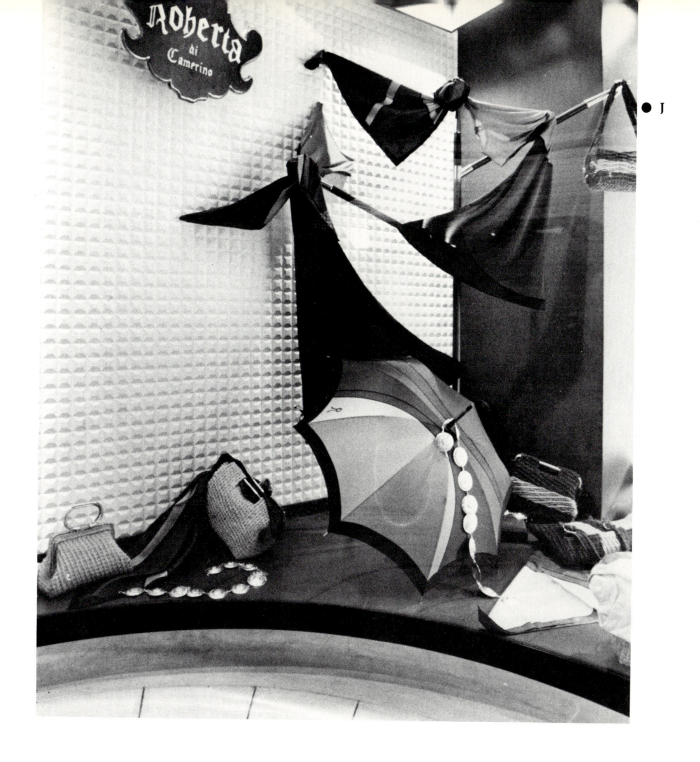

● J

29

● M

K ● Coming up with an innovative display for luggage is not easy. The New York specialty shop, Mark Cross, accomplishes it with almost nothing at all, except four suitcases of varying dimensions and some "happy smile" plates. The results are amusing, sophisticated and individual. Which is usually the kind of image an exclusive shop likes to project.

L ● As part of its presentation for the Givenchy Nouvelle Boutique, Harrod's Limited, London, takes the stark boutique display route. Very modern mannequins, stripped of all extraneous details, no props at all, and dramatic spotlighting are typical, but here the clothes also print the message.

M ● Characteristic of the way leather goods are shown in fine European specialty shops, Fendi-Vuitton, Rome, sets up a precise floor arrangement of merchandise—not too much, not too little, but just enough to convey simultaneously the message of exclusivity and excellent assortment.

3. children & young people

3. children & young people

Windows for children's clothes and the adolescent or young teen have come a long way from the corny and very cute. While elephants, books, Mother Goose and animal figures are still heavily used to say everything from "back-to-school" to "down-on-the-farm," new materials make such typical kids' props seem fresh and non-cliché. The young teen window has become especially exciting, often leading the way for new developments in Junior and sports clothes windows. Contemporary graphics, abstract shapes, lighting that borrows heavily from music festival "Light Show" techniques (colored gels, repetitive strobe, continuous motion, projected slide shows), have all helped establish a theatrical but relevant mood that young people respond to.

● A

A ● How many ways to spell out the alphabet? Bonwit Teller, New York, puts it quite simply with a spill of letters and a stark white relief of the alphabet rendered against a black wall. Merchandise is kept to a minimum for a crisp contemporary look to brother-and-sister outfits that manage to escape the •"too-cute" category.

For the Bonwit Kids, jumping from summer to school time is easy as A B C!

Young Ninth Floor

Playclothes fresh from Old MacDonald's Farm
Boys & Girls, Sixth Floor

● C

B ● Pinwheels, giant size, say "Liberi Tutti" — "Everybody Free" — for La Rinascente, Milan, in a multi-store children's fashion promotion. Otherwise, the window is handled very simply. Framed with curving cut-outs, figures are grouped asymetrically for a feeling of motion, with the old stand-by—balloons—heaped casually in baskets.

C ● While farm motifs appear again and again in children's windows, Bergdorf Goodman, New York, avoids overcrowding and overdoing by concentrating on the animal aspect. Mannequins are grouped closely together against painted animals in make-believe cages fronted with chicken wire. What's real are the piles of straw and genuine charm that emanate from the setting.

● D

D ● Down-on-the-farm again, the way a big city store sees it. Alexander's, New York, conjures up country atmosphere with some honest-to-goodness chicken crates, but fills them up with stuffed calico hens. The animals and crates come from Duplex Displays, Philadelphia; the kids could be from anywhere.

E ● Fantasyland doesn't necessarily mean a lot of expensive props. With some beautifully executed cut-out mushrooms set against black, a children's world is quickly established where denim is all dressed-up and kids keep snails for pets. John Wanamaker, Philadelphia, is responsible for this charming setting.

little loves for little loves by SYLVIA WHYTE
CHILDRENS SHOPS · SEVENTH FLOOR

● G

F ● The farmer's daughters bring their calico, charm and innocent airs to the city with some delightful reminders of their bucolic past. A striking wall hanging and quilted cow not only underscore the fabric of the clothes shown, but also establish "Farm" for B. Altman and Co., New York, without resorting to heavy realism.

G ● Clowns and kids seem to go together naturally. I. Magnin & Co., San Francisco, comes up with an especially appealing clown to establish a happy circus-y feeling for toddlers dress-up togs, and then throws in confetti and streamers for good measure. Nothing complicated, to be sure, but effective.

H

H ● Stix, Baer & Fuller, St. Louis, creates a fantasy forest for the young set with black netting hung at angles that somehow disappears magically into the background. What remains is a private world for children that's just fine for displaying a variety of new fashions for boys and girls.

I ● When realism works, it works very well indeed, as Saks Fifth Avenue, New York, demonstrates. A replica of a near-by historical restoration of colonial times provides fascinating background for some nostalgic girls' fashion to create display that's both interesting and appropriate.

CRAMER'S GENERAL STORE

OUR OWN HELEN LEE
VISITS SMITHVILLE

exclusively in our
Girls' Collection
Second Floor

SAKS FIFTH AVENUE

J ● Simply by building two enormous juice cartons, I. Magnin & Co., San Francisco, puts across sun and fun without relying solely on the usual beach props. Mannequins are also grouped in a fresh fashion for a natural, appealing look.

K ● Back-to-school without a book or pencil in sight. Bloomingdale's, New York, accomplishes this somewhat remarkable feat with a playful abstract of school bus in primary colors set against a clean black background. Mannequins are arranged closely together in delightful naturalistic poses.

44

L

NUMERO GESTIONE
105 U

SCUOLA

L ● Standa, Milan, designs basic back-to-"Scuola" windows that meet a variety of needs. Chrome tubes, polystyrene discs and black-and-white photo panel can be adapted to windows of all 212 Standa stores throughout Italy. They also permit display of often unrelated merchandise in a unified, non-confusing manner.

M ● A corner window gives Stix, Baer & Fuller, St. Louis, wide latitude for showing a lot of merchandise. Black is the background, while colorful wooden animals are arranged to add dimension and depth to the window. Animals also provide copy slant for tie-in with fiber people: "Mother's pet! New fall fashions of Celanese Fortrel from SBF!"

N ● Another excellent solution to the problem of showing a lot of merchandise with no common theme other than a new season. Lord & Taylor, New York, using far-out wooden beasts just for fun, hangs a number of different items quite frankly from lengths of wood and creates a forest of fashions for young people.

O ● A wall of sepia photographs taken from new and old favorite "flicks" checks out as super background for teen clothes with a nostalgic look. Gimbels, Philadelphia, also combines most effectively realistic mannequins and an amusing clothes rack in the same window.

"Check Mates"

Fashion Floor......The Third

● P

Q ●

50

"Short Dresses
With Lots Of Life"
by Denise

● R

P ● As part of a store-wide program "Making a New World," Thalhimers, Richmond, ties in teen fashions with "Make it Yourself" kits. At the same time it salutes Teen Board for their work in redoing a playground for under-privileged children. Blow-up in back of window reproduces teen-painted figures and art taken from walls of playground.

Q ● Indicating how misses' sportswear display has borrowed the paraphernalia and effects of the young junior customer, a brightly colored background is postered with "mod" figures. Mannequin is frankly young, with headband and long straight hair and for a Gimbels, Philadelphia, promotion of "What's New," clothes are changed daily to provide a wide view of "New, Young & You."

R ● With San Francisco as inspiration, Gimbels, Philadelphia, uses a specially-designed boutique trolley to house an eclectic variety of clothes and accessories for the young fashionable. A single interesting prop such as the trolley provides an excellent catch-all for any number of items.

the impact
of color

Pop statuary, essentially a simple hand of plaster, is all that's
necessary to make a knockout
summer window that's red, hot
and powerfully contemporary.
Designed by Hertie GmbH.,
Frankfurt, the giant hand could
easily be used with accessories,
kids' things, even as contrast
to very sophisticated evening
clothes.

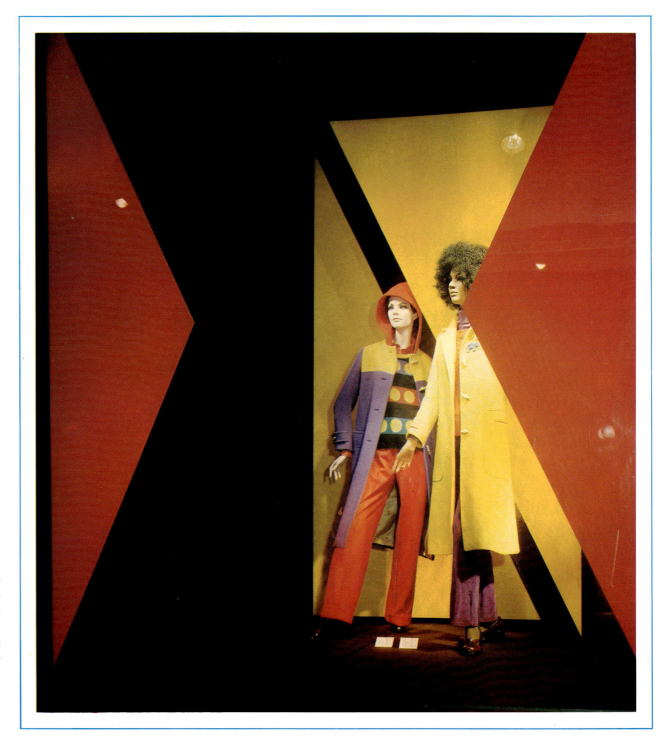

Framing a window with geometric shapes in primary colors, Macy's New York, makes graphics work as both eye-catcher and appropriate setting for the merchandise. Triangular shapes cut from plastic panels seem to pull the viewer into the window while pointing up the key colors of the clothes.

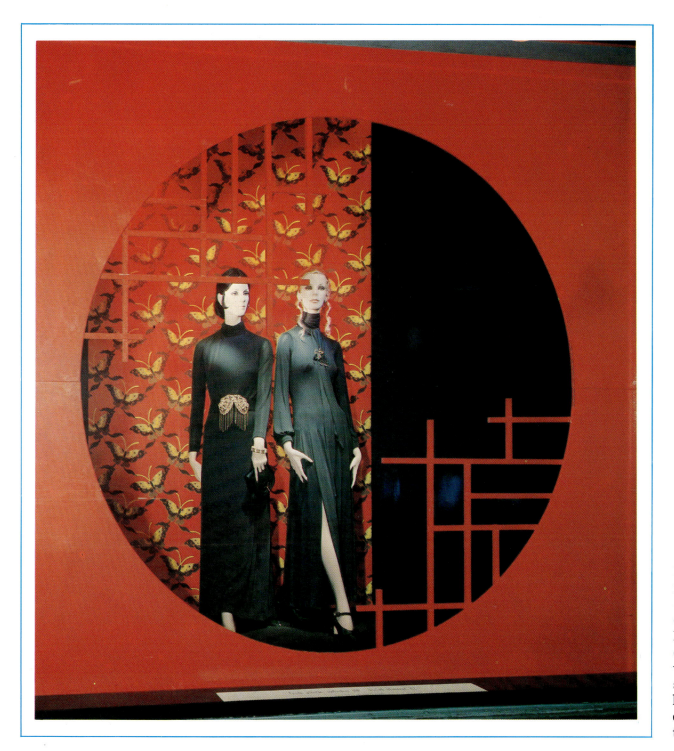

Building a dramatic and colorful window around two basically simple black evening dresses is not always easy. Bloomingdale's, New York, accomplishes it by framing in the window with strong graphic shapes and the addition of one high-key color — Chinese lacquer red — repeated in sumptuous background fabric.

Using the technique of many small boutiques, J. W. Robinson Company, Los Angeles, forgoes mannequins relying instead on mirrors and strategic lighting to create a contemporary clean-cut look for casual sportswear. Window copy makes an effective tie-in with mirror idea by talking about "Reflections '70".

ASIEN ZU GAST

Alsterhaus, Hamburg, establishes visually the source for its fabrics from southeastern Asia during an "Asia Week" promotion by the simple technique of a photograph blown-up window size. It continues the motif with bamboo logs covered with fabric and bolts of cloth draped in pagoda-like shapes.

A simulated sea of green creates an underwater fantasy for Horten AG, Duesseldorf. Mannequins are painted green to enhance the effect and the far-out headdresses bring the mermaid idea into this century.

One expects fantasy windows at Christmastime, but Saks Fifth Avenue, New York, goes all out with a never-never land that works as background for a wide variety of gift ideas and as a traffic-stopping vehicle. Twinkling lights, mirrored reflections, and the perpetual motion of a beautifully made puppet are sources of endless fascination to even the most casual passer-by.

How to celebrate a 75th anniversary and Christmas at the same time? Stix, Baer & Fuller, St. Louis, handles it effectively by forgetting about merchandise and creating a storybook institutional window that features a replica of its original store in a nostalgic holiday setting, peopled with authentic "customers" of the period.

4. fashion

palominos . . . corralled now
ts & Suits on three

4. fashion

By its very nature and definition, fashion is what's happening now. Fashion merchandise is the current, and in some cases, the coming thing. While fashion is a major selling force in home furnishings, furniture, children's clothing, men's wear, the word "fashion" is frequently used as a synonym for female apparel. Unfortunately, not all such merchandise qualifies as "fashion," nor does its window presentation. In fact, if the merchandise doesn't measure up as fashion—as newsworthy—it probably should not even be considered for display, much less actually be put in a window.

Assuming that the clothes or items do merit display, what emerges as characteristic of the genuine fashion window are several distinct approaches. In one, the presentation may be decidedly modern, even avant-garde, with sleeked-down, far-out mannequins in such contemporary materials as clear plastic or shiny synthetics. Another window may be pure fantasy, with an elaborate setting, exquisite props, innovative mannequins whose hair-do, makeup, attitude come from some never-never land. Or the window may be classic. Which does not mean stodgy. Far from it. Backgrounds are pristine, often black, always uncluttered. Lighting is dramatic. Usually a single, individual outfit is shown on a flawless mannequin, in some distinctive pose. Sometimes, there are two such outfits and mannequins.

In between these so-called "high fashion" approaches, there are varying degrees and types of fashion windows. Quite acceptable and often enormously interesting is the realistic window that reproduces a local scene that's "in"—bistro, theatre, bookstall, even a shop or boutique from within the store itself. Other fashion windows tie in with key fashion publications, or events such as a charity ball, benefit musical, sports match. Whatever the style of presentation, the goal is always the same: to achieve an atmosphere appropriate to the merchandise and conducive to its sale.

● A

A ● Modern with a capital "M". Against a highly contemporary work of art (borrowed), Saks Fifth Avenue, New York, sets a space-age, chrome-plated mannequin wafting out of the designer box. It all seems so simple, yet the window is composed as carefully as the painting it exhibits.

B

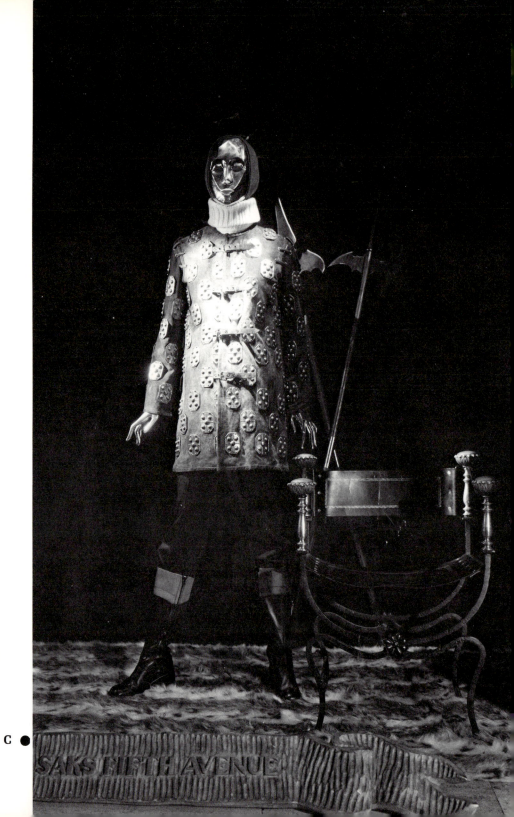

C

B ● Harrod's Limited, London, makes it modern with a stark white mannequin, black background, and a sheet of white plastic as foil for the accessories grouped discreetly on the floor. Otherwise, not an extraneous nail or doo-dad visible, except for sign scroll.

C ● What might be dubbed "zany modern." Sculptured mannequin in shiny armor and other appurtenances of knighthood reflect the medieval flavor of the clothes without getting 'corny' or too literal. Saks Fifth Avenue, New York.

D ● While not severely modern, John Wanamaker's raingear window for the Philadelphia store is still within the genre. Abstract mannequin, arty cut-out of flora and fauna, inky background—all in a tight little composition around the merchandise.

 E

Out of the
Art Gallery
into the Sun
with
Rose Marie Reid

E ● Although the mannequin is traditional, the mood of the window is modern. A single swimsuit is shown by The Halle Bros. Co., Cleveland, against modern shapes and designs that help underscore the clean-cut lines and print of the merchandise. Again, no extras.

F ● Classic the way Strawbridge & Clothier, Philadelphia, sees it. A subtle sprinkling of tiny lights on a black ground outline the impeccably groomed mannequin, placed front and center in the classic manner.

Bill Blass Prints
it for Spring!

TRIBOUTIQUE ON THREE

 G

G ● Going all out for graphics, John Wanamaker, Philadelphia, in no way diminishes the classic simplicity of a major fashion presentation. Just the other way around. The spare strong diagonals offer splendid counterpoint to the block dress design, to make a fashion statement that reeks of chic.

H ● Nothing fancy, yet everything about this window for Bonwit Teller, Cleveland, gives a feeling of good fashion. The designer signature blown-up is the key motif against black background and backs up a single mannequin in the classic manner.

● I

● J

I ● A classic presentation of an annual fashion event for Stix, Baer & Fuller, St. Louis. Interesting graphics spell it out and provide platform space for coordinated accessories. Newsy and newsworthy approach, only the fashions are now dated.

J ● A different kind of blow-up for Bonwit Teller, New York—Indian-inspired motifs—sets the mood for a collection of Indian summer fashions. Once again, a deceptively simple arrangement, beautifully lighted so that the entire emphasis is on the clothes.

K ● All the elements of the classic fashion window are here for B. Altman & Co., New York. The single striking prop (ceramic elephant) the fresh pots of flowers, black and white tile floor. But more than anything, the mannequin, reflecting the newest accessories, the most offbeat hairstyling, the most interesting stance makes a pure, undiluted fashion statement.

 L

L ● A little imaginative collage adds zest to a window for at-home fashion that could easily have turned out old-fashioned. I. Magnin & Co., San Francisco, keeps the look clean and contemporary, playing white against black and letting the clothes contribute the color.

M ● By the simple technique of posing the mannequin in a vigorous striding attitude, Bergdorf Goodman, New York, echoes the vibrant spirit of the clothes shown. The cutout backdrop also connotes a feeling of action, using contemporary shapes and patterns.

72

● M

Spring-spirited palominos . . . corralled now
in Coats & Suits on Three

Bonnie Cashin
Articulate Designs
Sculptured in Textures

N ● Dynamic duo. Two spirited mannequins capture the essence of a designer collection for Lipman Wolfe & Co., Portland. Even the rows of tiny lights seem to be alive. Yet that's all there is to the window—nothing extra or extraneous.

O ● Painted poles of varying circumference and strong spotlighting dramatize an otherwise simple window for Bullock's, Los Angeles Downtown. They also provide a nice feeling of dimension that seems to invite the eye right into the window.

74

The long and short of it!

Miss Bullock Shop, 3rd Fl. Hill St. Building
Collegienne Dresses, 4th Fl. Hill St. Building

Dress 100⁰⁰
Miss Bullock Shop

P ● A little razzle-dazzle lights up a collection of American Designer clothes for Lord & Taylor, New York. With the giant glittering letters (hammered metal) as background, a lineup of three mannequins works particularly well, reiterating as it does the designer hat, turtleneck and basic jacket looks.

Q ● If the clothes are colorful, put the background in neutral. Gimbels, Philadelphia, uses sepia-toned artwork to set off the high-key colors of a favorite designer, with not another prop in sight.

The Return Of
Rudi Gernreich
To Showcase 5

R ● Saks Fifth Avenue, New York, takes the passer-by into a realistic little bistro. Which, naturally, is just where one would wear the outfits shown. Even the lighting reflects the proper atmosphere.

S ● When The Halle Bros. Co., Cleveland, wants to promote its Halston collection, it simply reproduces a small vignette from the boutique in the store. Draperies, flowers, ceramic leopard are appointments typical of the designer and sum up his fashion point of view.

78

T ● Future shock. The Mitsukoshi Department Store, Japan, puts circles in squares and floats the mannequins upwards. The whole effect is dizzying, dramatic, and futuristic in feeling. And that was the whole idea.

U ● A stark Saks Fifth Avenue, New York, window that talks the language of fantasy with a floor-length wig for the mannequin while all else is deliberately black, frankly uncluttered. The effect is quite spectacular thanks to careful spotlighting, but more than anything thanks to that incredible wig.

V ● Peacock feathers, peacock colors, peacock print, even the peacock. How's that for a fantasy window at Bergdorf Goodman, New York, that really isn't as complicated as it sounds. Basically it's a single prop that does it—peacock and feathers.

● U

● V

W

W ● All the legendary charms of the Irish are incorporated in an Aquascutum Limited, London, window that borders on the fantastic. The merry-go-round horse is stripped antique pine, garlanded with shamrocks and Irish wildflowers. Mannequin is sleek and contemporary posed in an attitude of haughty elegance.

X ● Tying in with a current "hit" show, Saks Fifth Avenue, New York, uses it as a link to new fashion. Photographic blow-up wears an actual costume right off the stage; mannequin mimics stage pose to establish the fashion relationship.

FOLLIES,
THEN and NOW

in the Fifth Floor Shop

scenes from Lipman's
Wedding Album
with a heavenly collection of gowns for spring brides
Bridal Salon, 2nd floor . . . Lipman's

Y● Traditional bride and Z● contemporary bride. Lipman, Wolfe &
Co., Portland, Ore., does a romantic
setting, avoiding many of the usual
clichés with ethereal white branches
and a clean open feeling. Bergdorf
Goodman, New York, shows an un-
orthodox bride's dress in a modern
yet classic setting. White cut-outs
evoke images of Gothic church arch-
ways; the mood is one of serious
beauty.

5. home furnishings & furniture

5. home furnishings & furniture

Unless a store's specialty has been furniture or home furnishings, up to now, these items have been frequently relegated to side or back windows. Within the last decade, things have changed. More and more stores are devoting their most sought-after window space to the linen divisions (sheets, towels, bedspreads, table coverings), kitchenware, and furniture, as fashion has become a decisive force in these categories. With good design and attractive merchandise for inspiration, the window display has also grown more and more imaginative.

There are no set rules. Once a window designer has solved basic problems of reflections, lighting and color as it affects the specific merchandise planned for the window, anything goes.

● A

A ● Without going into a complete room setting, Bazaar Hotel de Ville, Paris, does a room in a window that manages to look complete while actually showing just a few pieces. The natural pose of the mannequin helps promote a feeling of "reality" as does the casual placement of accessories.

C ●

B ● Bullock's, Downtown Los Angeles, fills its window with a realistic room setting as part of its "California Mission Look" promotion. A corner window arrangement helps expand the room setting and provides continuity from every angle.

C ● The technique of using packing cases and shipping paraphernalia to set off new arrivals in almost any category of merchandise is invariably successful. Grand Magasin de Louvre, Paris, makes an interesting grouping of odd chairs around shipping crates which seem to heighten their newsy quality both from the aspect of design and of price.

D

D ● Sure, it's an old ploy, but done with some digression as Marshall Field, Chicago, does here, putting words into the mouths of paintings can be effective. The paintings are copies from the store's own galleries that seem to work well with the idea of antique-painted furniture. Sign copy follows through coherently: "Everyone's talking about it. The unpretentious elegance of painted cabinetry."

E ● Spanish furniture certainly offers many possibilities for an interesting window. Au Printemps, Paris, lets the merchandise speak for itself, relying on the intrinsic interest of a mammoth suit of armor for the key element. Moreover, since prices appear to be a significant factor, the store goes all out to make sure they're noticed.

G ●

F● When in doubt, hang it. Gimbels, Philadelphia, does just that in a Christmas home fashion window featuring bentwood chairs, caning, and other natural materials. Background is deep red, with stylized poinsettas pointing up the holiday mood. Copy pays off the "hanging" nicely: 'A real chair raising experience.'

G● While there is nothing new about a geometric theme, Bloomingdale's, New York, gives it fresh impact. Brightly-colored frames showcase a sparse arrangement of pillows far better, perhaps, than a window-full.

 H

H ● Marshall Field, Chicago, tackles the often difficult problems of glassware display, such as conflicting reflections and lighting, by covering units in dark blue felt and placing the merchandise on frosted glass units with indirect lighting. The pieces of crystal were obviously chosen with an eye to the overall window composition and shape.

I ● Wedgwood against stone cement blocks? Why not? B. Altman in New York creates what looks like a classic dinnerware window, but gives it a contemporary flavor by stark simplicity and tight grouping, using the blocks as both display platforms and unexpected texture contrast.

The Wedgwood Room

welcomes you with a wealth of your favorite dinnerware from England

fourth floor

J ● Another strong portrayal of graphics which figure prominently in so much recent home furnishings merchandise. Against a bold background of giant numbers in moss green, blue and yellow, a mix of contemporary lamps, pots, chrome tables, even rugs—somehow come together. Gimbels, Philadelphia.

K ● This time, it's the word, itself, that becomes the display. Bloomingdale's, New York, creates a strong graphic setting for casual tableware with giant dimensional letters that say it all. With the exception of a handsome barbeque, whose shape fills in for the missing "B".

L ● How to do a classy kitchenware window with a minimum of props. Strawbridge and Clothier, Philadelphia, works it out with rolls of shiny metallic stuff to establish the theme, and then lets the merchandise take over in an interestingly, seemingly casual jumble.

M ● Once again, the merchandise itself provides the key to window props and background. Beautiful porcelain animal figures re-state with elegance and sophistication the animal motifs in summer furnishings for Lord and Taylor, New York. Another uncomplicated and relatively inexpensive way (especially if they come from the store's own stock) to lend ambience to a basically simple window.

N ● With a lot of merchandise to display, Le Drugstore, Paris, utilizes a step-up arrangement of many little cloth-covered cubes, pulling them together with some far-out background that is indicative of the store's personality. A good way to separate and integrate at the same time, a variety of unrelated items.

O ● White Sale windows have come a long way from simply stacks and stacks of sheets and towels. In Philadelphia, Strawbridge and Clothier combines humorous line drawings with actual merchandise to add dimension and dash to what otherwise might have been just another display. So simple, yet so effective.

102

MAY LINEN EVENT
Savings for
Bed and Bath
on Five!

P ● What looks like art deco, turns out to be a magnified version of the actual sheets featured in the John Wanamaker, Philadelphia, "May Event." Although very little merchandise is displayed, the message of the window comes through loud and clear, thanks to the socko background and sophisticated grouping.

Q ● La Rinascente, Milan, does its White Sale window in a more traditional vein. While the presentation is straightforward, the merchandise is colorful and the use of a mannequin helps relieve the rows of sheets and towels.

R ● Who said White Sale windows have to be dull? Thalhimers, Richmond, does up a bath shop display red, white and blue, stopping traffic with a pair of provocative hands as merchandise stands. Actually, just a minimal amount of merchandise is shown, yet the impact is tremendous.

● Q

6. men's wear

6. men's wear

Window display for men's wear used to be divided into two approaches, basically. There were those who used realistic mannequins. And those who didn't. And those who didn't were usually the very conservative, frequently upper class type of store that relied primarily on headless, bottomless forms about which to drape the merchandise. As clothes for men changed, so have the techniques for their display. The majority of stores, even the most conservative, no longer hold to stiff dummies wearing the jacket with pants folded neatly to the side. In fact, some of the most imaginative window displays now come from the men's furnishing and clothing divisions.

A ● The temptation to fill up a large horizontal window with merchandise is usually very great—especially for the buyer or merchant. Instead, Bonwit Teller, New York, fills a men's wear window with galvanized pails of earth, some sprouting fledgling trees and shrubs, and some holding new casual clothes for men, thus establishing spring and men's clothing at one and the same time.

B● A window that oozes elegance and quality is created by Saks Fifth Avenue, New York, through the discreet emplacement of several expensive pieces of furniture, trompe l'oeil wallpaper background, and a classic arrangement of clothes without mannequins. The dinner suit is shown on a typical headless torso; one overcoat is thrown over a chair with apparent nonchalance; another is draped over library stairs.

C● Another view of elegance in men's clothing is projected by Bonwit Teller, New York, with a solitary mannequin, very realistically posed against a battery of phone booths. Everything about the mannequin and the clothes shown reflects a quiet air of quality, conservative but contemporary, including the obviously fine luggage and the reading matter spilling out of a bag.

C ●

111

D●Anything but conservative, a collection of snappy clothes is actually arranged in a simple manner by Austin Reed, Ltd., London. Using highly realistic mannequins that reflect the longer hair and sideburns of the moment, the store window takes its cue from the theme "Art Deco at Cue."

E●Featuring men's clothes from its Hermes' Boutique, Bonwit Teller, New York, builds a window around two male mannequins and empty paint cans. The former help establish the adventurous spirit of the new casual clothes for men; while the latter works as both striking visual element and a strong color tie-in.

F ● Aquascutum, Ltd., London, sets up a summer cruise promotion. Fishnet is stretched into sail-like shapes and completely covered with two-inch mirrored discs. More bits of the discs are used as flooring and both realistic mannequins and torso forms are used to good advantage.

G ● Brown wrapping paper stenciled with artwork in a taupe color becomes an effective background for a men's fashion window at Gimbels, Philadelphia. The build-ups are shipping cartons, proving once again how simple, utilitarian materials provide a quick, available, and interesting means to display merchandise.

H ● A handsome arrangement of men's furnishings takes the boutique route at Au Printemps, Paris. The basic torso form gets a face with an improvised scarf, and other men's accessories are carefully spaced around low contemporary screening.

I ● Another effective combination of contemporary male mannequin and still-life arrangement of merchandise is demonstrated in a corner window of Bonwit Teller, New York. By playing with simple wire hangers, the men's store here also indicates an imaginative approach to both clothes and the art of display.

I

J● With a stylized background of jungle motifs, Austin Reed Ltd., London, promotes "Safari" clothes for men. Using male mannequins whose stance, hair, and general attitude reflect the scene of the moment, the window speaks to the young fashion-conscious male of London in relevant terms.

K● When Austin Reed Ltd., London, wanted to reach an upper class customer for the launching of its "Pucci Room," it reverted to the classicism and "class" of the torso form on a stand. Window is simple, except for some contemporary Italian furniture and a typical Pucci print in the background.

K ●

L ● The men's store of Bonwit Teller, New York, continues to use natural-looking male mannequins as the prototype of the well-dressed, pace-setting, sophisticate they identify as their customer. Serving as a unifying element as well as dramatic interest, the network of roping also affords a clear view of the Hermes Shop within.

M ● Taking a traditional stance, Aquascutum Limited, London, does a Christmas window for men working against an antiqued-silver trellis set in front of shiny vinyl. Conservatively-groomed mannequins flank a large Regency pineapple covered with small mirrors and make-believe diamonds and pearls. The whole thing revolves slowly in blue spotlight.

N ● More than merely an attractive grouping of merchandise for men, a Saks Fifth Avenue window in New York projects a completely contemporary attitude that is also indicative of the clothes. A few well-chosen pieces of furniture plus a contemporary work of art on a fiberboard background are really all it takes. While the store opts for the conservative torso form, the sleekness and sparseness of the display evoke a mood that is thoroughly up-to-date.

O ● How many stores would dare to load a window with relics of the wrecking ball? Bonwit Teller, New York, does, thereby sustaining its image of the innovative and avant garde in men's clothing. A mustacheo'd male mannequin wears the clothes, with hair and overall attitude carefully fixed to echo the casual but sophisticated point of view.

7. seasonal, institutional, special events

7. seasonal, institutional, special events

Consider the quandary of display people who season in, season out are confronted with the same problem of creating original Christmas displays, saying "Mother's Day" another way, or vacation time, or back-to-school, or any of the recurring seasonal events that fill a merchandise calendar. Just how many new approaches are there to angels, Santa Claus, Fantasyland? Yet, each year they come up with still another new look, still another inventive make-believe world, still another ploy. Not only for Christmas, but also for special sales, magazine tie-ins, and all the various institutional-type windows that may show no actual merchandise but instead extoll some local event or community service. What helps, of course, are the constant improvements in techniques and the cooperation of display resources in their development. There is also a willingness to go far afield for unexpected materials, as well as maintaining a year-round alert for ideas from any source. The display person thinks Christmas in July (often a full year ahead), Spring in September, foreign expositions long before making a passport application.

 A

A ● One of Tiffany, New York's, classically beautiful windows marking Easter. A handsomely illuminated bible is framed symbolically with thorns and a lone lily plant, thus achieving visually what no words could possibly accomplish.

Picnic At The Bowl...
with Bach, Beethoven and Bullock's
Miss Bullock Shop 3rd fl Hill St Bldg

C ●

B; C ● An effective link between a seasonal concert series and Bullock's, Los Angeles Downtown, uses striking photographic blow-ups for background and all the accoutrements of what is apparently the customary picnic. Moreover, adding to the authenticity, chairs used in the windows were actually used by Mr. Bullock at The Bowl.

D● Saks Fifth Avenue, New York, notes the opening of The Kennedy Center for the Performing Arts with a dignified presentation in keeping with both the solemnity of the occasion and the high interest of a stratified social set. The window within-a-window provides the vehicle for an intimate, provocative display.

E● Magazine tie-ins can be notoriously dull—usually the magazine turned back to the page and that's it. Not the way John Wanamaker, Philadelphia, sees it. Here there's not a magazine in sight, yet with smart graphics and simple white board screening, a strong statement for both the fashion and the publication is made.

F● Gimbels, Philadelphia, creates a winning window for clothes, contest, and a store-wide theme "Walk Right in...Feel at Home," which appeared in all windows during this period. The background is scrim netting with an art portrayal of Piccadilly, London, applied in perspective.

G● Instead of relying on a flat poster and maybe one prop in order to do its duty to the community, Strawbridge & Clothier, Philadelphia, adds interest, depth and even a little drama to a small window announcing a local historical tour. Wrapping pictures around make-believe rockets is an idea that could be adapted to any Fourth-of-July window, with or without merchandise.

H● Proving one can promote the Navy and merchandise at the same time, Stix, Baer & Fuller, St. Louis, puts interesting art posters on the wall and classically lighted mannequins out front. Copy follows through with: "The fleet's in and SBF launches the fashion news for Spring."

● G

● H

● I

J ●

K ●

I; J ● A major local event, marking the centennial of the Civil War, gets major window display at The Halle Bros. Co., Cleveland. A whole bank of windows effectively depicted scenes and vignettes such as these, utilizing painted backdrops, moody lighting, mannequins authentically dressed in the style of the period.

K ● Celebrating the St. Louis Bi-Centennial with the community, Stix, Baer & Fuller builds out its windows to convert them into walk-in, walk-thru, old-fashioned shops. Removing the glass here, a corner window becomes the "Olde Tyme" ice cream parlor for the summer months.

135

 L

L; LL ● By the ingenious expedient of dramatizing the British flag with clever cut-outs, Strawbridge & Clothier, Philadelphia, establishes a thoroughly British atmosphere in a bank of windows remarkable for their impact. The cut-outs also lend themselves to skillful display of a wide variety of merchandise.

136

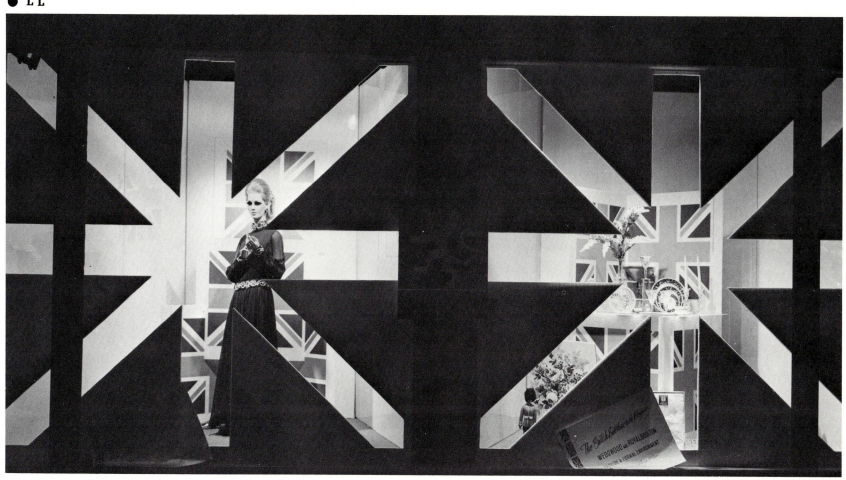

M ● As part of an Italian exposition, John Wanamaker, Philadelphia, puts some basic Italian in the window, stamps "Made in Italy" on the plate glass, and adds some packing crates for authenticity. Simple, yes. But it works.

N ● A traditional approach to an "Anniversary" window. Selfridge's, London, commemorates its Diamond Jubilee with a fabric presentation in delicate muted tones. Background is white moire, steps are white vinyl, flowers in and around white trellis framework are pale beige.

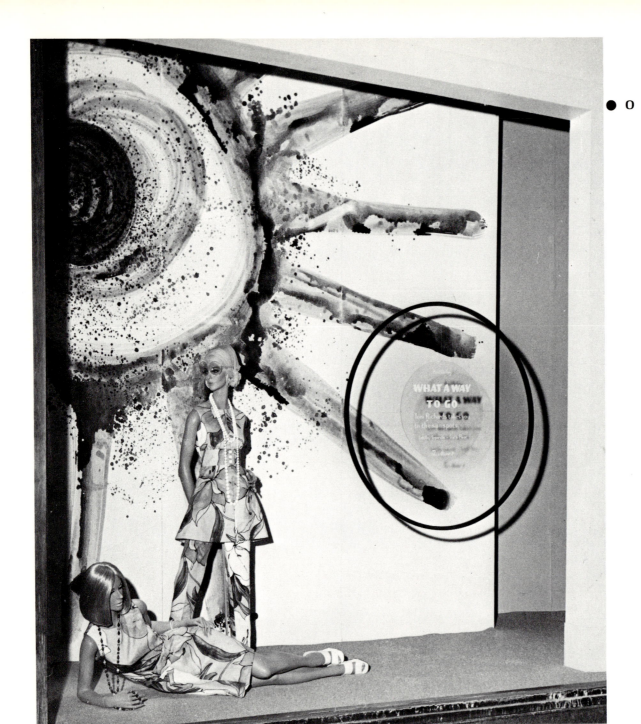

O ● "What a way to go" is the kick-off for a series of four Marshall Field, Chicago, cruise windows. Each window has a 4x12-foot panel for background, splashed with related but different free-form sunburst designs painted in hot tropical colors. The sign, suspended in a hoop, is executed in clear plastic.

P ● Standa, Milan, sets up a basic vacation display (that subsequently is picked up by all 212 Standa stores in Italy), built around a lifesize four-color photo panel and chrome tubes. Individual stores can then follow through with appropriate merchandise.

140

R ●

Q ● "My Mother," a poster combining photography and art work carries the Mother's Day message for all eight Gimbels stores throughout the Philadelphia area. Home accessories and gifts are displayed against a deep fuchsia background and distressed wooden platforms.

R ● Sometimes, it's what you don't see that counts. Stacks of familiar shopping bags promise all kinds of goodies within for an off-beat, upbeat sale window at Bergdorf Goodman, New York.

S ● Back-to-school and college pose new requirements each year. Marshall Field, Chicago, executes a series of 13 windows at 13 different shops to provide interesting backgrounds that are treated as miniature stage sets. Here, stylized white mannequins are posed in the barbershop, complete with real old barber chairs, sink, coat rack, and door. Background panels are from the 'twenties' and 'thirties.' Copy pays off in this way: "Enter the Seventy Scene with eclectic electives chosen from our Campus Quarters...."

T ● As part of the holiday-Christmas season, Gimbels, Philadelphia, commemorates Hanukkah, the Jewish Festival of Lights, which frequently falls within the same period. The background simulates a stained glass effect and a variety of unusual "Menorahs" or candelabras (which hold the traditional candles) are grouped in the window.

T ●

146

U ● Lining up ski windows, The Halle Bros. Co., Cleveland, puts the tow to work. An interesting effect that could also be adapted (with appropriate panels such as Voting Booth, Telephone Box, etc.) for other merchandise and seasons.

147

V ● Using a different "material" as theme (iron here), Marshall Field, Chicago, provides the basic theme for 10 different Christmas windows, exhibiting 10 different categories of gift-y merchandise. Each is framed with authentic barn siding and natural twigs turned into a wreath-like shape. Other materials spotlighted, with appropriate backgrounds and props include wood, pewter, brass, glass.

W;X;Y;Z;AA ● Some of the Christmas fantasy and storybook windows as developed by major U.S. department and specialty stores. **W** Saks Fifth Avenue, New York, in a frosty land of exquisite gifts, presided over by a cavorting footman. **X** A Victorian never-never land, one of a series of fantasy windows created by B. Altman & Co., New York. **Y** From Stix, Baer & Fuller, St. Louis, a traditional corner window display with Santa and helpers set in motion mechanically. **Z** "Once upon a time" becomes the magic fairyland for Christmas at Marshall Field, Chicago, where princes, swans, deer, and mannequins wearing crowns, live throughout the season. **AA** "Christmas at Versailles" is depicted in a series of Christmas windows at The Halle Bros. Co., Cleveland, with model rooms reproducing much of the splendor of this famous French palace.

w

● Y

● **Z**

● **AA**

BB ● Bloomingdale's New York, wraps up Christmas in a completely contemporary fashion with an exhibit of 25 graphic posters, touting its 25 holiday-geared special shops. Merchandise noted ranges from clothes to toys. Posters are grouped within a red felt-covered, mirror plastic-lined frame, shaped with tiny lights.

152

153

8. tricks of the trade

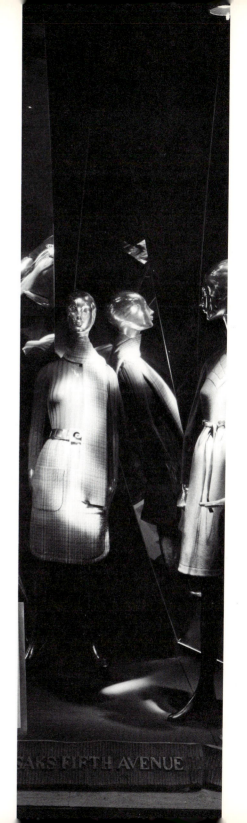

8. tricks of the trade

Many store people think that lack of money and a small display department (or none at all) inhibit the development of exciting window display and merchandise presentation. By now, it should be clear, nothing could be farther from the actual facts. Ordinary materials make the most extra-ordinary windows. Five-and-dime stuff can make a million dollars' worth of jewels look like two million.

A single contemporary mannequin, including hair-do and attitude, can do more for a store and its merchandise than a window crammed full of new fashions, stuck on yesterday's mannequin figures. It would seem fundamental that it's not how much money one spends on props and background that determines the success of a window. It's rather where the money goes and for what. It's a few basic investments in good spotlights, an up-dated mannequin, several pair of inexpensive but current shoe designs (to dye a hundred times if necessary) so that even the shoes look right—although it's dresses you may be selling. It's a willingness to paint the floor of a window, again and again, to set a new and different mood for each new and different display. It's the gumption to borrow and beg good art, a striking piece of furniture, unusual antiques to lend tone and atmosphere to a window. In sum, it's energy. And imagination. And attention to little details that add up to an impressive window.

Essentially these are the tricks and the techniques of the "trade" that are the mark of a professional.

A

A ● With the simple expedient of stage-type lighting, a dramatic window is born. Stix, Baer & Fuller, St. Louis, lights up fashion headliners from Vogue Magazine with vertical and horizontal bands of glowing bulbs, keeps everything else clean and spare.

B ● An easy approach to graphics involves translucent letters and designs to hang any number of ways for a floating effect. Gimbels, Philadelphia, uses the device for back-to-school windows, keeping floor and background shiny white. The idea of see-through letters can be adapted for almost any kind of merchandise.

C ● Instant forest. Bergdorf Goodman, New York, does it with sturdy cut-outs, arranged to give a feeling of dimension to the window. Once again, black proves best for background. Cut out trees could be made of heavy cardboard or wood, painted whatever real or fantasy colors that would work best with the clothes.

D ● What could be simpler than bonafide bamboo poles to frame a fashion window? Leaning in all different directions, they are neither static nor stiff, are easily obtainable, and can be propped up with wires, wall, or glue. Lord and Taylor, New York, arranges them here against stark black.

E ● Gimbels, Philadelphia, takes advantage of materials at hand. Shipping department foam board was cut, silk inserts applied, and voila — a striking backdrop (weighing only a half pound all told) for both dresses and accessories.

E

"Short Dressings
For Great Nights"

Fashion Floor . . . . . The Third

G ●

F ● High fashion without high cost. Even without dividing the window as B. Altman & Co., New York, does here, the effect would be elegant and expensive-looking. What helps accomplish it are the exquisite tub vases, filled with fresh (note—*fresh*) flowers, and set on unusual carved stands. Many antique shops are quite willing to lend choice props like these as long as credit is given somewhere in the window with a small card or sign.

G ● No, not real, but the effect is. Some clever sleuthing could turn up equally dramatic animals to provide atmosphere for either a fashion or children's, or in fact, most any kind of window. Bergdorf Goodman, New York, uses these classy hounds for a big-city window that would be striking with or without the dimensional backdrop.

H ● Who said you had to spend a fortune for a dramatic window display? With just a few simple abstract shapes in bright colors and a witty hand-stand to hold the window sign, John Wanamaker, Philadelphia, makes a strong fashion statement. The added fillip of a suspended paint can pouring pretend paint is more difficult to execute, but within the talent range and capacities of most.

I ● Admittedly, not everyone can afford to commission pop statuary for display purposes, as Hertie, G.m.b.H., Frankfurt, does. But when one has the resources available, it's a worthwhile investment that can be amortized in any number of interior and exterior displays, for a wide variety of merchandise.

J ● With the budget and facilities of a big-city specialty shop at its disposal, Bonwit Teller, New York, still opts for the unexpected use of down-to-earth material (and nothing more) in a window for men's casual clothes. A roll of wrapping paper unfurled and then crunched up offers all kinds of interesting possibilities.

I ●

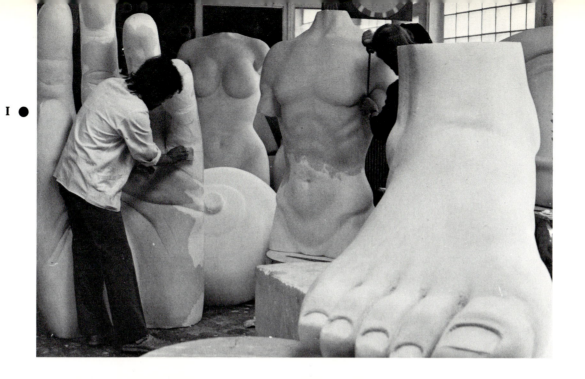

J ●

K ● The device of a painted backdrop, which is used so effectively in stage settings as well, offers endless potential for a provocative but easily executed window display. Here, Gimbels, Philadelphia, puts it to work as a reflection of current young culture, painting it in a monochromatic scheme of raspberry, pink and red, with "mod" figure motifs. Pop the merchandise in front, and that's it.

L ● There's more than one way for a designer to "sign" in. In Cleveland, Bonwit Teller sets up a Scrabble board and says it all. Certainly, the idea of such a board and any words it spells out could work with any merchandise category, fashion or not.

M ● Butterflies are practically free. Something Japan's Mitsukoshi Department Store demonstrates very well with colorful cut-outs that can be developed in many motifs. Western-style mannequins establish clothes from the "Elle Club," whose name is printed right on the windowpane itself.

N ● Blow-up at Bergdorf Goodman, New York, for the introduction of the Biba look from London. Sepia blow-ups of the merchandise provide all the background that is needed, while the actual dress photographed is hung on a charming clothes rack. The use of photographic blow-ups, providing the photograph is well-done, can establish a window mood quickly, simply, and relatively inexpensively.

better every day!

Boot-ique

our fabulous collection...

Shoe Salon . . . . Street Floor

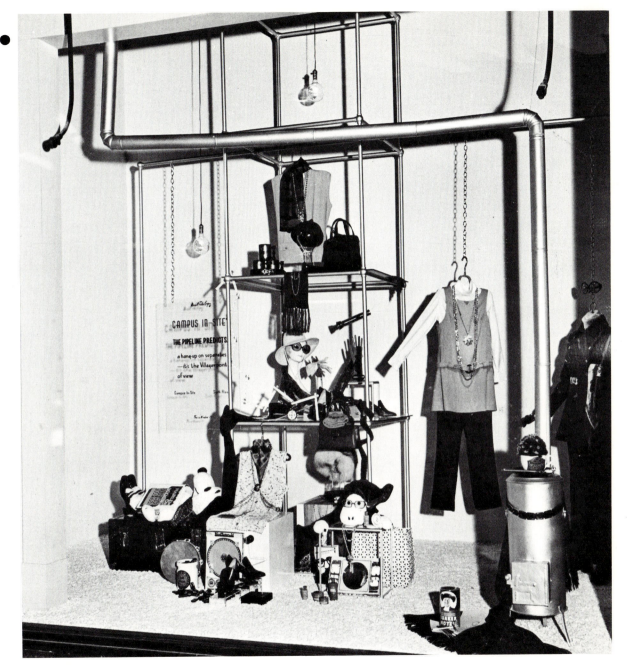

O● Invest in one well-designed chrome module unit and you have the wherewithal to display a wide variety of accessories, shoes, housewares, and so on. Gimbels, Philadelphia, creates a Mondrian effect with boots and related accessories, against grooved walls of natural wood.

P● Marshall Field, Chicago, makes its own display module, using basic plumbing and stove pipes, something most any store could adapt not only to provide a set-up for accessories but as background to fashion, other merchandise. Copy follows through nicely here: "The Pipeline Predicts...."

R ●

Q ● What do you do with all those 'empties'? Fill up a window with them to make a statement about "Summer Refreshment" or "It's the Real Thing" or whatever works in context with the merchandise and the kind of bottles shown. Bonwit Teller, New York, platforms clothes from its men's store with empty Coke bottles while a view of the Hermes Shop within provides the background.

———————————

R ● Although not always easy to execute, mirrors in a window can give display a new slant and merchandise fresh perspective. Saks Fifth Avenue, New York, effects some particularly spectacular mirror magic, using odd shapes, placing them at strategic angles, and spotlighting sleek modern mannequins from above. An idea worth experimenting with.

173

S ● To be sure, sugar cubes are a natural for silver sugar spoons. But how many stores would use the real thing, filling up a small window the way Bergdorf Goodman, New York, does for its fine jewelry boutique? The point being: feel free to rob the kitchen cupboard or any of the down-to-earth supplies readily available and use them 'en masse' for really dramatic effects.

T ● A tower of empty wooden thread spools works particularly well in a glassware window for Tiffany, New York, not only because of the paradox of everyday material against fine glass, but also because the shape of the spool echoes that of the glass. Thus, it's not enough to toss in ordinary stuff as foil for elegant merchandise; the disparate components still have to work together.

U; V ● Any hang-ups about using such mundane materials as wire hangers should be dispelled here and now. Bonwit Teller, New York, handles hangers two ways. With jewelry, they function as both design motif and something from which to hang merchandise. In a small window showing cigarette lighters, the hangers become a design device, whose shine and shape backs up the copy statement: "Aflame with excitement...."

S ●

T ●

Make it a dazzling Bonwit Christmas! Jewelry, First Floor

U

V

W ● An optical illusion that requires no costly props to accomplish — only an innovative eye. Credit Strawbridge & Clothier, Philadelphia, with the originality and courage to break rules by turning a bedspread window upside down. Not literally. All it involves is visualizing the room upside down, and then arranging bed, furniture, and furnishings to simulate the effect.

reflections

Hopefully, it should now be apparent that some of the most exciting window displays are frequently the most simple.

That merchandise should be fresh, current and newsworthy to be worthy of window display.

That an up-to-date, well-made mannequin may be the most important investment of a store or display department.

That the use of unexpected materials, out of context, and in juxtaposition to seemingly unrelated merchandise, can elevate a display to star quality.

That window copy should pay off a visual idea, and vice-versa.

That money is not necessarily the key ingredient. What is—is left to your imagination.

about
SHIRLEY JOEL

Big store, little store, department or discount store, specialty shop, boutique—there's almost no type of retail operation that Shirley Joel hasn't had some working experience with. Born, bred, schooled in Boston, Mass., she graduated magna cum laude from Boston University, majoring in journalism and advertising. In Boston, Mrs. Joel was chief fashion writer at Filene's, involved in windows, fashion shows, and of course the advertising. Later in New York, when husband Yale Joel, the well-known photographer, was transferred to the Life Magazine office there, she moved on to Abraham & Straus and subsequently B. Altman & Co. Then came a stint at Batten, Barton, Durstine & Osborne, advertising agency, where she became a copy group head on the Du Pont account, concentrating primarily on ready-to-wear areas, teen, better fashion, hosiery, and intimate apparel. She later joined Saks Fifth Avenue as Advertising Manager for all stores, winning an Andy "Honorable Mention" Award in 1968 for a small space institutional advertising campaign she conceived and executed for the store. At Saks, she was involved with display as well, working closely with the display department. In between there were three children, (two boys and a girl) several dogs, a house in the country north of New York City, and almost a year in Paris on a house-exchange program. Currently consultant to a number of fine stores, Mrs. Joel is also deep into the audio-visual area, developing and writing educational and training programs, mixed media sales presentations, and related film programs.

acknowledgments

Where does a publisher begin? Of course, with Shirley Joel, the editor, and Dick Kluga, the designer. But those are the "sung"—as opposed to unsung—heroes of the effort. They will be on display—with the exciting windows—on the cover and title page.

But hundreds who played more modest roles will only be noted in the paragraphs that follow. And undoubtedly, some worthy souls will be slighted due to human failing, no doubt mostly ours.

A fervent salute to Nick Malan Studios which specializes in window display pictures in the New York area. Almost nobody but nobody doesn't use Malan in New York. So the heavy preponderance of material from Manhattan and environs bears the Malan stamp.

But scores of other photographers and photo services are represented, and these deserve special mention: Chicago—Loren Kelley Photography; Cleveland—Childress Studio; London, England—Mason Bryar Studios Ltd., Atlas Photography Ltd., Roger S. Randall; Los Angeles—Warren Bowen; Mesquite, Texas—Paradeses Photo Service; Mill Valley, Calif.—Davis; New York City—Retail Reporting Bureau; Portland, Ore.—Photo Art Commercial Studio; Richmond, Va.—Dementi Studio; San Francisco—Cal-Pictures.

A low bow to Fairchild Bureaus throughout the United States, and especially, Fairchild staffers heading foreign bureaus—in London, Paris, Rome, Milan, Frankfurt and Tokyo—for helping make this book a truly international experience. At great risk, we'll single out these Fairchild colleagues: Adriana Grassi, Bob Reehling, Don Whittaker, Bill Raser, Bernie Leason, John Fujii and Jake Fuller. And add editorial people from Fairchild Books: Donna Fyler, Shelly Ruchlin, Marjorie Lewis.

But the people who made this book possible were the people who made the windows possible.

We're crediting all of the creators and inspirers below. If anyone is left out, it's because we didn't know about them. The listings are chapter-by-chapter. Second mentions will be compact—last name and store identity.

This has been a labor of love and anguish. It has, we feel, ended happily. We believe this book will be a classic of its kind—thanks to all those mentioned above and below.

E. B. Gold, Mgr.
FAIRCHILD BOOK DIVISION

There must be a special note of thanks to the countless fine stores who emptied their files for us, knowing that many of the photographs might never see the light of print, and to their staff, display and others for their enthusiastic cooperation. In particular, an extra thank-you to Henry Callahan, Vice President and Corporate Director of Visual Merchandising for Saks Fifth Avenue, and Louis Guariglia, Display Director of the New York Saks Fifth Avenue, for sharing with me many of their thoughts on the entire subject of window display.

Shirley Joel
Sept. 1972

ACCESSORIES AND COSMETICS

A John Spetter, Display Director, John Atkinson, Window Designer, Betty Winters, Fashionist, **Bullock's**, Los Angeles.

B & K Ivan Minderhout, Executive Vice-President, **Lipman and Wolfe & Co.**, Portland, Ore.

C Thelma Malloy, Display Director, **Neiman-Marcus**, Dallas.

E B. H. Doroff, Executive Vice-President and Sales Promotion Manager, **John Wanamaker**, Philadelphia.

G Gordon Ryan, Display Director, **Bloomingdale's**, New York.

I Nancy Gunn, Display Director, **Livingston's**, San Francisco.

J A. Van Hollander, General Display Director, **Gimbels**, Philadelphia.

M Pierre Lalire, Director of Design and Merchandise Presentation, **The Halle Bros. Co.**, Cleveland.

O Virginia Paxson, Display Manager, Shelley Christensen, Window Designer, **Marshall Field**, Chicago.

Q Joseph Miller, Display Manager, **Macy's**, New York.

R H. I. Callahan, Corporate Director of Visual Merchandising, **Saks Fifth Avenue.**

THE BOUTIQUE APPROACH AND SMALL
SPECIALITY SHOP

H Doroff, **John Wanamaker**, Philadelphia.

CHILDREN'S AND YOUNG PEOPLE

B Giancarlo Ortelli, Display Division Director, **La Rinascente**, Italy.

E Doroff, **John Wanamaker**, Philadelphia.

G & J Ray Wills, Display Director, **I. Magnin & Co.**, San Francisco.

H & M Ron Brummel, Director of Design and Display, **Stix, Baer & Fuller**, St. Louis.

L Athos Vicentini, Director of Display Design, **Standa**, Italy.

Q & O & R Van Hollander, **Gimbels**, Philadelphia.

P Kip Kephart, Window Director, **Thalhimers**, Richmond.

FASHION

D & G Doroff, **John Wanamaker**, Philadelphia.

E & S Lalire, **The Halle Bros. Co.**, Cleveland.

F Robert N. Mattis, Display Director, **Strawbridge & Clothier**, Philadelphia.

H Thomas Randleman, Display Director, **Bonwit Teller**, Cleveland.

L Wills, **I. Magnin**, San Francisco.

O Spetter, Atkinson, and Winters, **Bullock's**, Los Angeles.

Q Van Hollander, **Gimbels**, Philadelphia.

W Mike Moore, Display Director, Michael Southgate, Window Designer, **Aquascutum Ltd.**, London.

FURNITURE AND HOME FURNISHINGS

B Spetter, **Bullock's**, Los Angeles.

D & H Paxson, and Tom Elliott, Window Designer, **Marshall Field**, Chicago.

F & J Van Hollander, **Gimbels**, Philadelphia.

G & K Ryan, **Bloomingdale's**, New York.

K & N Mattis, **Strawbridge and Clothier**, Philadelphia.

O Doroff, **John Wanamaker**, Philadelphia.

P Ortelli, **La Rinascente**, Italy.

Q Kephart, **Thalhimers**, Richmond.

MEN'S WEAR

D & J & K Ron Dyer, Display Controller, **Austin Reed Ltd.**, London.

G Van Hollander, **Gimbels**, Philadelphia.

M Moore, and Southgate, **Aquascutum Ltd.**, London.

SEASONAL, INSTITUTIONAL, AND
SPECIAL EVENTS

B & C Spetter, Atkinson, White, and Winters, **Bullock's**, Los Angeles.

E & N Doroff, **John Wanamaker**, Philadelphia.

F & R & V Van Hollander, **Gimbels**, Philadelphia.

G & L & M Mattis, **Strawbridge & Clothier**, Philadelphia.

I & J & U & BB Lalire, **The Halle Bros., Co.**, Cleveland.

P & T & W & AA Paxson, and Barrett, **Marshall Field**, Chicago.

Q Vicentini, **Standa**, Italy

Z Brummel, **Stix, Baer & Fuller**, St. Louis

TRICKS OF THE TRADE

B & E & K & O Van Hollander, **Gimbels**, Philadelphia.

H Doroff, **John Wanamaker**, Philadelphia.

L Randleman, **Bonwit Teller**, Cleveland.

P Paxson, **Marshall Field**, Chicago.

V Mattis, **Strawbridge & Clothier**, Philadelphia.

THE IMPACT OF COLOR

F Brummel, **Stix, Baer, & Fuller**, St. Louis.

H Richard Donley, Display Director, M. Manninen, Window Manager, **J. W. Robinson Co.**, Los Angeles.

index